DOG-MOM
Nike's Bernese Mountain Dog Tale!

by
Roger Hite

(Photos by Debby Hite)

Also by Roger Hite

The Nun of Camelot (2011)*
On My Mind (2011)*
Oregon Love (2011)*
From Groundhog Day to Camelot (2010)*
I Still Buy Green Bananas (2010*
The Return to Marlboro (2010)*
Unwrapping Christmas (2009)*
Last Stop before Paradise (2009*)
The Marlboro Incident (2009)*
Buster's View (2009)*
The Loser (2008)*
Buster's Spirit (2008)*
The Iron Butterfly (2008)*
Nesting Among Ducks (2008)*
Cottage by the Sea (2007)*
The Foul Game (2007)
The Five Dollar Fortune (2006)
Vivid Imagination (2005)
The Sister Deal (2004)
The God Switch (2004)
Soul Merchants (2004)
Buster's View (2002)
Mirror Man (2001)
Buster Back at the Wall (2001)
The Twelve Candle Miracle (1999)
What's the Good Word? (1999)
The Ebony Snowflake (1999)
The Art of Awe (1998)
Our Gift (1998)
Buster at My Side (1997)
Buster at the Gate (1995)
Buster at the Wall (1994)

*Still Available In Print

Dedication

To Buster, Toby and Luke—three Golden Retrievers who gave thirty-years of unconditional love and the courage to acquire Nike and to continue with a new dog adventure—and to Blue, the Standard Poodle who lived next door for a decade and who had a fondness for our Luke! And to Watson, the Bernese who caught Debby's eye and introduced us to the Bernese Mountain Dogs.

[Toby (left) and Luke with me at our special place on "the wall" at Rio Del Mar in Aptos, CA]

Preface

I am blessed to be married to a classic "dog-mom." Like many women who have a natural, maternal instinct driving them to fulfill their gift of motherhood by birthing and raising two-legged human "puppies," dog-moms are blessed with another passion. Many dog-moms add dog-raising to the everyday tasks and responsibilities they have in addition to raising human children.

Some, like my wife, do not have human children—either by choice or circumstances—but who nonetheless have a maternal role that focuses on raising "four-legged" children.

Ask any dog-mom without human puppies and they will tell you the dogs are indeed their "children." They make no apologies for treating animals with the same degree of love and concern women have for natural born children.

Dog-moms face a reality unlike what moms face when they raise human two-legged puppies. A dog-mom knows her children will never grow-up and leave the security of mother's love. They do not venture out on their own adult adventure. Dog-moms know it is inevitable they will outlive their own children. They will see their children grow, mature, and die—all within a relative short life-span compared with humans. Dog-moms know from the time they welcome a puppy into their family, they will be faced with the reality of telling the vet when it is their child's time to become an angel!

I begin with such a grim reality, not to cast this book as a tragedy—as this book is a joyful celebration of the first-year of our Bernese Mountain Dog's adventure. I point out the fact because in the case of all dogs—especially large breed dogs—life is all too short. It is, however, one of the simply realities all dog-moms face. It takes a strong woman to devote much of her life and nurturing love to raising a puppy in the face of such realities.

Dog-moms will probably raise several generations of four-legged children during the course of their own motherhood. That has certainly been the case with my wife.

It was the case when it was our time to once again make the choice on June 23, 2010 to put down our aging Golden Retriever, Luke.

(This is a picture of Toby (left) and Luke (right) standing on our balcony in Aptos, California waiting for me to arrive home in the evening)

Like the reality we faced with our previous four-legged children, we had to selflessly let go of an infirmed dog and allow him to go to where God takes dogs at the time of their passing.

Many dog-mom's grieve so deeply at the time they let go of a four-legged child they make the promise most almost always break: "I'll never be able to own another dog!" Many don't say "never" but make it clear they will need at least a year to grieve through the loss.

When we put down Luke, Nike's dog-mom was sure it would be many months—perhaps a year or more before she would be ready to re-assume a dog-mom role again.

Then, as often happens, grieving dog-moms do what they know they will inevitable do. They gather the courage of motherhood and take the risk of considering a new relationship.

This book is not about our current dog-child Nike, or about our past Golden Retrievers—Toby or Luke or Buster—it is about dog-moms—and not just Nike's Dog Mom.

It is about the nurturing behavior human female's display toward four-legged animals in search of food, love, and companionship.

Somewhere in the past eons of time when humans began experiencing the unfolding of God's Grand Scheme of Things, a primitive woman stooped down and cradled a trembling puppy in her arms and shared her body's warmth and some morsels of food she was preparing for her hungry family who were also gathered around the open fire.

It was at that precious moment when God created Dog-moms! And, they have existed ever since—through millenniums of human wars and tribal strife. Dog-moms have kept alive dogs that may well have fallen prey to extinction through natural selection processes or through consumption of their flesh by human carnivores.

The book begins with the realization that a dog-mom's passion and love for animals is the genesis of a story that is now unfolding again with our new four-legged "child."

Nike's dog-mom grew up in a rural farm area in Northern California. From the earliest days of her own childhood, she learned how to form responsible, loving and nurturing relationships with animals. She had a lamb, dogs, horses, cats, chickens, and an array of stray creatures she found in the fields and ditches around her home. She made a pet cemetery that symbolized the reverence this future dog-mom would have for all forms of animal life.

When Nike's dog-mom moved away from home and the rural community in which she was raised, she had a brief hiatus from four-legged relationships. She finished her education and undertook her own professional training. If the truth were told, this dog-mom's top priority was to become a veterinarian. However, she was told vet school was not woman's work so she refocused her caring compassion on a profession that allowed her to help injured humans back into productive lives. For thirty years she pursued her career as an occupational therapist.

When Nike's dog-mom finally reached her early thirties and was well-established in her career, she married her first husband. It was not a story-book beginning for her human relationship and perhaps because she sensed all was not right, she opted to focus her maternal instincts on acquiring a four-legged child.

That was when she became an official dog-mom and adopted into her human relationship a Golden Retriever puppy. Buster became the love of her life and the source of her support as her human relationship with her former husband continued to suffer.

When Nike's dog-mom's first husband lost control of his will to live and took his own life, her relationship with her four-legged child saw her through the challenging difficulties of loss and recovery.

It was a couple of years between her former husband's tragic death and the time she and I started dating. When we did become an "item" Nike's dog-mom made it very clear to me that "love me, love my dog!"

In retrospect, it was an easy agreement to make. I quickly fell in love with my wife's dog child. He and I formed a close loving relationship. It lasted for almost six years before we had to tearfully watch as the vet put Buster to sleep on the floor of our home where we lived for the last years of Buster's life. The home was an easy evening's walk down to the beach where Buster and I would spend some of the best years of our relationship sitting on the brick beach wall talking about all the things that mattered in life, love and death.

I wrote my first book about that relationship and published it under the title, BUSTER AT THE WALL: A Golden Retriever Looks at Life, Love, and Death.

My relationship with Buster allowed me to experience first-hand the loving bond that occurs between a dog-mom and her four-legged children. Buster was indeed, my wife's child in every sense of the word. Before long I was talking like a dog-dad as well—even though I had some experience in raising two sons in my previous marriage. I didn't have a parent-child relationship with Buster. It was from the get-go an adult-to-adult friendship. He became for me a friend and companion, and a literary vehicle for me to see the world from the perspective of an animal.

I used my relationship with Buster as the impetus to continue on with my fledgling writing career. I was more than a bit pre-occupied with my realization that the dog-mom to whom I was married was facing the reality that her aging child was soon going to meet his maker.

To help cushion such a reality, I continued on with the second book in what was to become my "Buster Trilogy." I wrote a fantasy story about Buster dying and going to heaven, only to discover dogs were not allowed past the Pearly Gates. BUSTER AT THE GATE was my way of trying to soften the reality that Buster was going to no longer be present in our family.

When the time came to put down Buster I told that story in the final book of the trilogy—BUSTER AT MY SIDE. Even though the book documented the events that led to our decision to put down Buster, it was uplifting. There was also a tragic episode in dog-mom's life. We adopted through a Golden Retriever Rescue organization a beautiful Golden named Rou. Sadly, we did not realize that Rou was a biter—a rare occurrence in Golden Retrievers. We learned of his problem when he snapped at Dog-

mom's young nephew and bit him in the face. Fortunately, the wound was below the eye and there was no permanent damage.

When we did further inquiries with the rescue agency, they did follow-up with the family that had turned in Rou and learned he indeed had a history of aggressive behavior.

Dog-mom was faced with the reality that Rou had been a part of our family for only 40 days. Now she was going to have to return him to the rescue agency so they could euthanize him!

Dog-mom resisted and politely told the agency she would keep the dog in quarantine and would herself take Rou to our local vet and be present in a loving way when he was put to sleep!

I thought the task of supervising Rou's demise would traumatize Dog-mom and drive her away from any thoughts of ever getting another Golden Retriever.

I was wrong, of course!

Not long after the terrible, tragic loss of Rou, we connected to a local breeder and adopted another Golden Retriever named Toby.

We acquired Toby when he was returned to the breeder after six-months. The family that purchased Toby bought him for their daughter. He was apparently left alone in their yard unattended much of the time. The family was going through a divorce so when the papers were filed the husband arranged to return Toby to the breeder.

Toby turned out to be quite a challenge. It was not long after we acquired him that we moved into our new home. For the several weeks in the new house we did not have the back yard fenced with a dog run. That required us to leave Toby in the garage during the day when we were at work. He was frustrated and gnawed daily at the garage door—scratching the surface and symbolizing his need for daily companionship.

Toby was unruly and acting out to the point Nike's dog-mom was beginning to think it had been a mistake to acquire a dog so soon after the loss of Buster and the tragic episode with Rou. That was when we decided to see if a companion dog would solve the problems with Toby.

It did. Toby became almost maternal in his care and concern for Luke—the tiny little golden ball of fur we brought home from the breeder one afternoon. He was such a joyful addition to our family.

For the next eight and a half years Toby and Luke were inseparable. They enjoyed each other's companionship in our spacious back-yard dog run while Nike's dog-mom and I were working at the hospital during the days. In the evenings and on weekends we devoted time to building our relationship with the dogs.

Eventually, the time came when cancer crippled Toby and we once again made the decision to release a Golden child and continue on with only the presence of Luke. It was again a tearful, grieving time for us. Luke suffered with us as he was aware of the fact he would now bear greater responsibility to fill the void left by Toby's death—though in retrospect he seemed to love the attention.

A couple of years after Toby's death we made the decision to move from our home in Santa Cruz and venture up into Oregon to a new home. We worried if Luke would be up to the transition. He was a large dog and we wondered how he would adapt. Our fears were soon set aside.

For almost two years Luke was a vital part of our Oregon adventure. Then, in the early summer of 2010, we were once again faced with the decision. Nike's dog-mom was beside herself as she watched her third golden child approach death. When we took him to the vet's for the final visit, it was a painful experience for us to again let go.

There is perhaps no sadder experience than to helplessly watch a dog-mom struggling to let go of a former child and at the same time wishing she would find a new relationship to fill the void.

Luke died in June.

In early October Nike's dog-mom came home from a visit to a local home improvement store. She was all excited at having seen a beautiful dog waiting in a car for its master to return from the store. I could tell something was stirring in dog-mom's mind and heart.

Dog-mom explained that when the other dog-mom returned to her car, she introduced herself to the woman and they talked about the dog and the breed.

I was surprised to learn it was not a Golden Retriever—but a Bernese Mountain Dog. I learned that the breed had its origin in Berne, Switzerland. It was noted for its beautiful tri-color black, rust-brown and white fur. It was bred to be a working farm animal—noted for pulling carts that farmers used to carry supplies to the marketplace or on the farm.

The dog's name was Watson. His dog-mom was a retired school teacher who lived in Eugene.

Nike's dog-mom called the breeder and it was only a matter of a few days before she was making her inquiry about whether a litter of puppies might be available in the next fall?

Much to our surprise, we learned a litter was scheduled to be born in four days! If Nike's dog-mom wanted a Bernese Mountain Dog puppy, one would be available in mid-December—almost six-months ahead of dog-mom's schedule!

It didn't take long for us to agree that it was time for Nike's dog-mom to become a dog-mom again. When the puppies were born and three weeks old, we drove from Eugene to Vader, Washington to the country home of Beverly Search, the breeder. We met Holly the mother of the litter and examined the puppies.

I took several pictures of Nike's dog-mom and the puppies and we affirmed that Nike's dog-mom was definitely ready to become once again a dog-mom.

For the eight weeks between the birth and the weaning age of the puppies, Nike's dog-mom behaved like any soon to be mother. We bought the right supplies and did the things to puppy-proof the house. It was almost like preparing a nursery for a new baby!

When the day finally arrived for the drive up to Vader to pick up our new four-legged child, there were some last minute expressions of angst and concern that maybe we weren't ready—maybe a Bernese would be so much different than a Golden we wouldn't be satisfied.

If I shared such concerns with the anxious dog-mother to be, I had my fears and doubts erased almost immediately after we drove away from the breeder's home. I was driving our van and Nike's dog-mom was in the back seat holding Nike. He had already grown substantially from when we first saw him as a puppy. He was now almost twenty-two pounds.

During much of the three and a half-hour drive back down I-5 to Eugene, I had to bat back tears of joy. I kept stealing glimpses of Nike's dog-mom in the rear view mirror holding and cuddling her new baby! I guess it was appropriate to say I was like a proud new father watching for the first time as the new child nestled next to his mom!

For much of the final years of our Golden Retriever's lives, people would see the white faces of the old dogs and stop me with the inquiry, "How old is your dog?"

From the moment we made our first rest-stop along I-5 to let puppy Nike out to do his business, people began to stop and admire him. "What a beautiful little dog. What kind is he?"

Such inquiries seemed to be the rule rather than the exception as we began to take Nike on walks. Wherever we took him people commented on his beauty! And it hasn't changed now that he is almost a year old and approaching a hundred pounds in weight.

When he was younger people would always gasp when we told him he was only a puppy. They would look at his huge paws and roll their eyes, exclaiming, "Look at the size of them! He's going to be huge!" Then in the very next breath they would say, "What a beautiful dog!" Even today, we seldom walk Nike without someone exclaiming "he's beautiful!"

I soon realized that unlike the relationship we had with our three previous Golden Retrievers, Nike's dog-mom had a different thought of the adventure we were undertaking with Nike. Instead of having him fixed at six-months, she wanted to enjoy showing him off and perhaps allowing him to be studded when he is mature enough—especially if he continues to display such remarkable show-qualities that are beginning to manifest in his development.

Nike doesn't know he is a show-dog. He is like all our other four-legged children from the past years. He looks at us with his playful, almost defiant eyes and only wants one thing from life—our undivided attention and admiration and love when he wants.

Unlike our Golden Retriever puppies, Nike is so much bigger as a puppy than the retrievers were. It is often necessary for me to step back and remind myself that he has a puppy brain inside what is more than an adult-size body of most large dogs. He is still a puppy at heart.

In much of the literature we have read and studied about the Bernese Mountain Dog we recognize the lifespan of this breed is much shorter than smaller dogs and perhaps shorter than our previous Golden Retrievers.' One source said it best when it cautioned us: Think of the Bernese in terms of three stages of life: two years of challenging puppy life; two years of awesome, mellow years of middle-life; and, two years of older dog challenges. In short, be prepared to have a wonderful life with the animal, but realize it will be a relatively short lifespan.

We will hold such knowledge in the recesses of our minds and do our best to relish each day of Nike's live span—however long or short it may prove to be.

This book is about the first year of Nike's life. It is about the affirmation of how Nike's dog-mom has re-awakened the spirit or a dog's unconditional love in our family life.

It was befitting that Nike was the Christmas gift my wife and I gave to each other in 2010. Now as we approach Christmas of 2011, it is fitting to share with family and friends and fellow-dog lovers the story of what we experienced during this first year of our "new child" adventure.

We continue to believe Nike is an absolutely handsome, strikingly well-bred animal. He is a true family member—as much so as if he had been born of human flesh. His joy and well-being is one of the great focuses of our current life.

Nike is our first potential wannabe show-dog! It is a dimension of his life I have mixed feelings about. If we continue to show him, I will have to learn how to be a responsible, respectful participant in such a world. The world of breeding and dog shows is indeed a world unto itself. It is not for the faint-hearted. If anyone ever wished to have a real-life laboratory to study normal and abnormal behaviors in dog-moms, the dog-show is the perfect venue.

I hope that the pictures and the text of the stories that follow will allow me to do justice to all the curious and interesting things we experienced in the first year of Nike's adventure. I have resisted putting captions under each photo as I think each captures the spirit of the moment. Nike's Dog-mom is a talented photographer and graciously allowed me to peruse through the hundreds of photo she took of Nike during this first year of his life.

There is one thing I think will surface for people who read through the following pages: Nike may not ever reach the pinnacle of a world-champion in the critical eyes of those who make such judgments for a living as professional dog-show judges.

There should be no doubt, however, that his dog-mom ranks among those who are truly world-class!

Nike brings out the best in his dog-mom!

1

Training Nike

A smart dog-mom knows when to get professional help—whether it is a vet, a groomer, or a dog trainer and show-dog handler. She will spare no expense, sacrifice whatever is necessary, and behave as though the dog is the center of her universe—because it is!

The first few weeks with Nike in his new home reminded both Dog-mom and I what it was like to have a puppy present in the household. Everything is a new adventure for the puppy. There are no boundaries and everything is a game of snatch and run. A paper napkin on one's lap at the dinner-table will disappear as the stealth thief dashes for the back door with his contraband!

Dog-mom was elated by the joy of having a four-legged child romping once again around the household. She didn't even mind the equivalent to the two-am feeding in which the puppy indicated he needed to go out and do his thing. The occasional accidents that brought out the high-powered dog spot removal cleaning agents didn't disrupt the joy of her new motherhood. Even when the puppy chewed on her favorite shoes and darted down the stairs with items from her closet she suffered with a smile as she corrected his behavior.

Some puppy behavior was more difficult to swallow than others. It was a nuisance when Nike chewed the fingers off of Dog-mom's best gardening gloves. It was equally annoying when he dug in parts of the yard he wasn't supposed to disrupt. I was especially annoyed when he went into the front room and stole the television channel remote control and left it in ruins on the backyard grass near his favorite nesting place under some trees. I was pushed to the brink of beating Nike when he went into my study and purloined my computer mouse and chew it beyond recognition—again leaving it on the back yard lawn.

Dog-mom was not exempt from Nike's mischievous behavior—all designed to gain attention by what we presumed was a "bored" puppy. Nike snatched Dog-mom's expensive bird-watching binoculars during one of his "counter-surfing" ventures—and chewed them so they were practically useless.

Nike was and has remained a "handful" for Dog-mom and me during this first year. We keep reminding ourselves, however, that he is still a puppy in what is more than a normal adult-sized dog body!

Unlike Dog-mom's former experiences with the Golden Retriever puppies, she could see from the very start that the stubborn, playful, head-strong tendency of a male Bernese Mountain Dog (BMD) was more consequential than a Golden. Nike quickly learned to overwhelm Dog-mom's good-hearted tendency to give her child the benefit of the doubt and to allow him to run on a long leash.

Fortunately, Dog-mom is a woman of great patience when it comes to raising her children. Despite his errant behaviors, his barking when he is jealous that Dog-mom is conversing with someone and ignoring him, Dog-mom is quick to succumb to the love and affection Nike shows towards her.

Dog-mom created and continues to use several terms of endearment for her four-legged child. If she doesn't call him Nike, she will often use the affectionate term "Big Guy" or "The Kid" or "The Puppy." Whatever the moniker, they are all used interchangeable and with love. Whenever we are displeased with something he does, we playfully refer to him as "Your Dog!"

A walk through the neighborhood with Nike taught us both that a BMD had a mind of his own and wanted to take control of any walk. Dog-mom tried to be patient as she used various types of leashes and collars. Now that he is approaching his full mature size, Dog-mom is reluctantly switching to a pinch collar instead of the slip chain collar—as the slip chain collar was wearing the coat in a way that will detract from his showing, and, more important, it doesn't make him as responsive as a pinch collar.

Nike, on the other hand, continued to insist on having things his way. The tug-of-war contests were more easily controlled by Dog-mom during the first couple of months. But as Nike grew in size and strength it became obvious that unless he was well-trained as a puppy, he was going to be unmanageable as a larger, more mature dog that would eventually weigh-in in excess of 120 pounds.

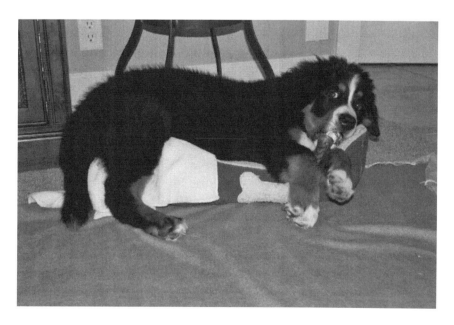

Dog-mom was also observing habits and trends she had not experienced during the raising of her golden children. Dog-mom loved to roll around on the living room floor and engage her child in playful puppy wrestling and play. Nike was in the midst of teething and he had no concept of how powerful his mouth and teething was when it came to chewing playfully on Dog-mom's arms and hands. Soon, frustrated Dog-mom's arms and hands looked like they had been a chew-toy for a playful puppy.

In addition, the tiny, almost razor sharp puppy teeth were finding surfaces throughout the house and out on the back porch to chew on to alleviate the teething sensations. Dog-mom got products to spray and apply to furniture legs and to spread chewed upon spots, but it was much more of a challenge than it had been with the other four-legged children. She finally discovered that Vicks vapor rub could be applied to a surface and it seemed to effectively deter Nike's chewing behavior.

Then, as though as it was the last straw on the list of inappropriate puppy behaviors she had not experienced with the Golden Retriever children, Nike had managed to wrack-up a lot of negative points for his habit of barking—almost as though as he was trying to protest and declaim whenever he had a contrary opinion about something he wanted or something he didn't want to do that was being commanded by dog-mom!

What was most annoying was Nike's habit of barking whenever Dog-Mom was talking over the fence with her sister who is our next-door neighbor in Eugene. Nike was jealous that somebody other than him was the focus of attention of Dog-mom!

In all her years as a golden dog-mom, Nike's dog-mom never had to deal with a jealous, attention craving, and barking dog.

Finally, one afternoon, almost in frustration, Dog-mom exclaimed, "I need to find someone to help me train this guy before it's too late!"

I agreed with her observation and we turned to the phone book. There we found an advertisement for the Ken Schilling Dog Training Academy. We dialed the number and left a message. Hours later we were on the phone with Ken who told us he would take a look at Nike and give us an assessment. We arranged to drive out to Ken's rural farm in nearby Noti—a small community fifteen miles from Eugene.

It was an overcast, misty afternoon when we arrived at his place. We were somewhat surprised at how remote Ken's place was and evening questioning if we were at the right place.

When we pulled into an open area behind a one-level ranch style home there was a sign that indicated we were indeed at the Ken Schilling Dog Facility. I rolled down the van window and spoke briefly to a short, bearded man wearing a down vest and a cowboy hat. It was the owner Ken Schilling. I immediately realized he was a man of few words as I explained we were the folks who needed some assistance training their Bernese Mountain Dog puppy. He nodded and motioned to us to park our van nearby the open area.

When we got out, Dog-mom had Nike on a leash. He was eager to explore all the grounds, but also mindful that there were many German Shepard dogs in nearby kennels and some goats and chickens wandering around the open area near a barn.

Dog-mom took the lead and explained all the problems we were seeing with Nike and how we needed help in training him before he became too large to manage given our current limited knowledge of training such large animals.

Ken listened politely to Dog-mom and didn't say a word. Finally, when it was appropriate he rubbed his chin and explained in as few words as possible: "If you want to know the source of your dog's behavior problems, all you have to do is look in the mirror. You're the problem."

Dog-mom was not especially appreciative of such an observation but was willing to continue listening as Ken took Nike and attached a long thin yellow cord-rope to his collar. He then showed Dog-mom how to use the cord to correct the movement and the behavior of her child. He also told her that a spray bottle with some water and a few drops of centranella could be used to stop Nike's habit of barking.

Before the mid-morning consultation visit was over, Dog-mom was convinced this soft-spoken, low-key man really knew his business. She agreed that we would sign-up Nike for some training classes. Even though Nike was several weeks shy of Schilling's minimum age for dog training, given Nike's size, he seemed willing to bend the rule and allow Nike to participate.

On the way home we stopped at a feed store that sold the centranella. Schilling also gave us advice on the kind of collar we should use that would allow us to better communicate with the dog's brain through quick sharp tugs on the leash. We also purchased a long cord so we could see if it would assist us in training Nike to come when we called him in the backyard..

A couple of weeks later we attended the first night training at Schilling's store-front training center—a space he shares with an Archery Club on 11th Avenue in Eugene.

That evening there was a woman who signed up for the ten week cycle of his beginning dog discipline training program. Unlike the rest of us who initially crowded into the small office with our dogs to sign up, she left her unruly dog in her car—fearful of how he would behave in the office.

After we all signed up, we were escorted out to the adjacent parking area next to the building and back off the busy roadway. There Ken lined up the dozen or so new dog owners and allowed his son to begin taking us through their basic exercises.

Dog-mom took charge of being on the human side of the leash to Nike. I leaned against the wall in the cold evening and watched. I was most struck with how shortly after the class began Ken Schilling came from the front of the building with the most unruly, almost hostile dog struggling and fighting in a frenetic manner at the end of the leash.

The class was interrupted for several minutes as the rest of the dog-moms and their dogs watched Ken perform his techniques on the angry, combative dog. In less than ten minutes Ken had the dog heeling and obeying his commands! It was almost as though he was a bare-back rider who had mounted a spirited un-tamed colt and ridden it into tranquil submission. I later told Dog-mom that I had never been so impressed with an animal trainer's skill than I was that evening. If anybody could help us train our stubborn, head-strong Nike, Schilling was the man!

For several weekends we dutifully climbed into the van and made our drive over to 11th Avenue in the evenings to put Nike through the one-hour training and discipline with a dozen other dogs. In addition, on Saturday mornings we drove out to Ken's place in Noti and joined with a group of fifteen to eighteen other dog owners in a one-hour training program.

Dog-mom was pleased with Nike's progress with basic training and she learned several things to work on each week as we returned home and went through the rituals of training and daily living in our own neighborhood.

All the while we worked on training Nike, Dog-mom maintained regular contact with Beverley Search, the breeder who lives in Vader, Washington—the person I playfully called She-Who-Was-the-Source. I simply now call her "The Source."

It seems like a respectful, proper moniker inasmuch as she was both the source of the dog as well as the source of all knowledge about the habits and likes/dislikes of the breed. As the challenges of being a Bernese owner presented themselves to Dog-mom, so did the strength of her relationship with The Source.

The Source had a not so hidden agenda when she selected Dog-mom to raise one of her dog's puppies. The Source selected what she thought was a show-quality animal when she sold us Nike. The Source wanted us to make sure we didn't have Nike fixed for at least the first year so we could determine if he had all the qualities necessary to make him attractive for breeding. We agreed to such a condition when we picked up Nike in mid-December of 2010.

Dog-mom continued to pick the brain of The Source during the first months he was with us so we could understand what to expect from a growing male Bernese. During these frequent e-mail exchanges and occasional phone calls, The Source connected Dog-mom with her handler who then connected Dog-mom with an organization in Eugene that trained wannabe show-dogs and their owners on how to participate in showing the dog in competitive dog shows.

Dog-mom was intrigued by the idea and wanted very much to show off her handsome animal in formal competition. Like any proud owner who had a well-bred four-legged child, Dog-mom was eager to learn all the ropes.

I went with Dog-mom the first time she went to the class. It was held in the National Guard Armory in Springfield during the early evening hours. I was impressed by how cordial the trainers were and how supportive they were of the notion they could help non-professional dog handlers learn the skills necessary to enjoy the experience of taking their animals through the routines of a dog show.

Dog-mom was all excited after her first couple of sessions and when she spoke with The Source she received encouragement as well. However, The Source explained that the local shows were good training for the owner and dog and certainly would be helpful in preparing Nike for the large dog shows. She told Dog-mom that if she really wanted Nike to do well in the big shows, it would be worth the expense to contract with a professional handler to make sure he was displayed with the best show and discipline possible.

Dog-mom accepted such wisdom because it did not preclude her from entering the fascinating world of show-dog competition on a low-key basis.

After some modest levels of training in the procedures, protocols, and basic techniques for showing Nike, Dog-mom took the big leap and entered her handsome child in some real competition.

On April 17, 2011 Silvertip Lord Nike made his debut as a show-dog at the International All Breeders Canine Association's show held at the Eugene Fairgrounds facility.

Dog-mom was more nervous leading up to the event than I had ever seen her in the twenty-some-years of our marriage. She was determined to make sure she and Nike did their best. What she wasn't expecting was how the whole adventure finally turned out.

(Why are you frowning, Nike!? Don't you know you're Swiss and Are supposed to love snow—however infrequently it falls in Eugene!)

2

The Premier Showing

When Dog-mom told me the dates of the Eugene dog show I was hesitant to tell her I wouldn't be able to participate—at least not on the first day. I was obligated to participate in a mediation session with a local federal district judge who had volunteered his time to assist an organization in which I was on the board resolve a serious issue that had rendered the board paralyzed in its own decision-making process.

Dog-mom was unwavering in her support of my decision to not attend on Saturday. But it was like not being at a human son's first little-league game—a feeling that somehow I was letting down the family. I knew, however, I could attend the second day of the show and would at least have the experience of watching Dog-mom show off our handsome child and put him through the ritual and routines required to judge his conformity to the breeding standards of Bernese Mountain Dogs. I would also be able to see how well he competed with other breeds in the four-to-six month age bracket.

When I returned home that evening Dog-mom's face was still flush from the ordeal Nike had put her through at the dog show that Saturday.

I poured Dog-mom a glass of wine and we both sat down in the front room. Nike was sprawled out on the floor, his legs protruding in frog-like fashion behind him as he positioned his head between his front paws and rolled his eyes up so he could watch both Dog-mom and me carry on our conversation.

Dog-mom was beside herself and didn't know exactly where to begin her story. Finally, she blurted out—"I decided that even though things didn't go well today, Nike and I are going back for the show tomorrow. I decided we can't do any worse than we did today—and it will be good experience for both Nike and me."

I looked at Dog-mom and smiled as I innocently asked, "What happened? It sounds like Nike didn't perform well?"

Dog-mom took another deep breath, and started her story from the beginning.

"When we got to the Fairgrounds I found out that the show was being conducted indoors where they usually show horses and other animals. Instead of being on a tile floor, the surface was dirt."

"Was that a problem?"

"Well, after I registered Nike and it was my turn to take him into the ring, I put on his little handler collar and leash and led him to the edge of the ring. The moment he put his feet into the soft powdery dirt a little puff of dust rose as he placed his paw on the dirt. That was all it took!"

"What do you mean?"

"Nike was delighted at the powdery experience! All he wanted to do was cavort and enjoy the dirt instead of attend to business. He got so excited he finally leaped into the air almost to my eye level before landing and continuing to prance around in the dusty floor covering!"

"What did the judge do when he acted out?"

"She was very patient with me and allowed me to exit the ring with Nike and to take him to where he could get calm. I told her that maybe he was excited because he had to pee! Which of course wasn't the case! All he wanted to do was play in the dirt!"

I could tell Dog-mom was bewildered at what she could have done differently. For several weeks she had gone to class and received tips on how best to handle her four-legged child when he was being shown.

"So, are you telling that you're giving up on Nike's show career after one time on stage?"

Dog-mom's jaw locked and she looked at me sternly.

"Absolutely not! We're going back tomorrow. It's a whole new show and there will be a new judge."

"Good for you guys," I said glancing down at Nike and then back up into the determined eyes of Dog-mom.

"It wasn't a total failure. When we got back in the ring after the false start, Nike actually did a pretty good job. At the end, the judge took the time to fill out her papers and she explained to me that his physical structure and appearance met and exceeded all of the standards for a Bernese puppy."

Dog-mom looked down at her child and a smile came across her face.

"We're going to get back on the horse that threw up, aren't we Big Guy!"

Nike rolled his eyes as if to acknowledge, "Whatever!"

He then closed his eyes and pretended to be totally disinterested in whatever Dog-mom was saying to me.

I stood up and motioned to Dog-mom, "Come on, let's take Nike for a walk before dinner. I'll tell you about all that happened in the mediation—although I already know it will be nothing as exciting as your morning and afternoon."

* * * * * * * *

The next morning we got around and Dog-mom loaded The Kid into the back of the van and we drove down to the Eugene Fairgrounds. It was a kind of overcast and threatening gray day that promised to water the area with some showers before the afternoon was over.

When we arrived at the parking lot Dog-Mom realized that in all the hustle to get around we had left some of the entry papers on the kitchen counter. I told Dog-mom to relax. I said I would keep Big

Guy outside on a leash and walk him around to get him calm while she went inside and straightened out the entry registration without the papers.

When Dog-mom was in the building re-registering Nike for the competition, I walked him around the paved parking lot and down to where there was some dirt where he could pee!

We returned to the area outside the entry door and watched as several other owners paraded various breeds of dogs into the entrance door. I looked down at Nike and had a heart-to-heart talk with the Big Guy. I told him I expected him to be attentive to Dog-mom and not act unruly as he had done on the first day. I finished my little sermon with the admonition I always gave my own two-legged sons before they competed, "Remember who you are and who you represent."

I knew that the only thing Nike probably heard was "blah, blah, blah." But it made me feel good I'd done my part to get us off on the right foot! And, as it turned out, there was sufficient evidence the little talk did make a difference!

Moments later Dog-mom came through the door with a nervous smile on her face. The paper work was straightened out and he was entered in the classes she had chosen. I handed her the leash and said I would return to the van to get her camera. I wanted to capture in images whatever he did in the ring with Dog-mom.

After retrieving the camera I made my way into the huge enclosed arena building and located Dog-mom and Nike. They were sitting in the first row of the wooden bleachers that ran the length of the massive dirt floor.

I had absolutely not a clue regarding the protocols and procedures of how a dog show operates. What did strike me as I looked around the building was how serious many of the dog handlers were about grooming and preparing their animals for the show. Several very serious looking women had small dogs posed on a grooming table so they could be brushed and their coats made ready for the show. Hair dryers were a common sound as one passed by the grooming area. There was a smell of hair spray in the air! For many, this was serious business.

The moment I sat down in the dog show venue I sensed what Dog-mom felt about the place. Unlike the cool tile floors of the National Guard Armory, the dirt was certainly an unnecessary distraction for the animals. I wondered, too, how the serious faced owners who were grooming white poodles felt about having their meticulously groomed dogs prancing through the two inches of powdery dirt.

Several minutes passed before it was time for Dog-mom to lead Nike back into the show area for his class. When it was time for his turn, I positioned myself with a folding chair on one far side of the rectangle arena that was fenced off appropriately for the dogs and handlers to display their merits.

I held my breath as Dog-mom entered the competitive arena and began following the direction the judge. A proud smile spread across my face as I watched in disbelief. Nike was a model performer! He went through the routine and protocol as though he were a veteran of several shows—not merely a competitor with one prior show experience!

At the end of the first class, Nike was awarded a blue ribbon. Dog-mom was elated with their success. I thought the contest was over—only to learn there was more to come. He had to advance to another level of competition—which he again performed well and won. When I prepared to leave I again was told to relax. Nike was now eligible for the best of breed puppy competition for his age.

In the final competition Nike was awarded Best of Show Puppy Reserve Champion. He was given a pink and purple ribbon. It was tantamount to second-place runner up status. It was a huge ribbon and Dog-mom could barely contain her prideful emotions as she accepted the ribbon.

Nike didn't seem to care, one way of the other. Instead, he was more interested in chewing on a fancy dried chewing treat that someone gave him after he won.

One of the dog show instructors was a big help to Dog-mom that day. She was herself a trained judge and quite knowledgeable about dog show protocols. She told Dog-mom that Nike should have actually won the blue ribbon for the over-all class champion in the puppy division. I have since learned that such condolences are often shared by friends of those who come up short in the final judging.

There was not a prouder person on the face of the earth than Dog-mom! We put Nike on his leash and led him back to where we parked the van. He hopped into the back and quickly settled down into his crate. He was exhausted from all the excitement of the show. He rolled over onto his side and was snoring softly not long after the van rolled out of the fairgrounds parking lot heading home.

I could tell Dog-mom had visions of Westminster dancing in her head as she talked about preparing her winner for the next showing. It was at that moment I realized that we were going to have to let this new adventure into dog-showing run its course!

3

The Albany Adventure

Dog-mom was elated at her success in showing The Kid on the second day of the Eugene show. As soon as we returned home Dog-mom was on her computer e-mailing The Source with the good news about Nike's turn-around performance.

It didn't take much for Dog-mom to follow the advice of The Source. She was told that it was good warm-up for the big show in Portland in mid-July. The Source—being a competitive breeder who liked to win—advised Dog-mom that if she wanted to really have The Kid do well it would be worth the investment to connect with a professional handler.

Dog-mom was easy to persuade—even though she liked the idea of being the owner-handler, her brief experience in Eugene taught her it was a stressful activity—and one she could afford to hand off to a professional.

The Source had already connected with Dog-mom with the woman who was successful in showing several of the Bernese Mountain Dogs that were a part of The Source's family. Dog-mom agreed and made arrangements to take The Big Guy to a show in Albany where The Handler was showing one of The Source's kids.

Given the fact that Nike was only four-months old and considered a puppy, The Handler wanted to have a look at him so she could judge for herself whether he was suitable for serious young dog competition at the larger AKC shows.

The experience at the Eugene dog show did not excite me enough to warrant volunteering to go with Dog-mom to the event. One show was sufficient to fully satisfy my appetite. Dog shows are not my thing—but I needed to be respectful of Dog-mom's ambitions for Nike.

Dog-mom left early in the morning for the 45 minute drive from Eugene up I-5 to Albany. I got around and saw them off on the next step in Nike's dog show career. He wasn't being shown, but the trip would allow Dog-mom to visit with The Source. It would also give Dog-mom a chance to see one of Nike's sisters and, most, important it would allow her to meet The Handler and give her a chance to size up Nike and to determine if she would agree to train him and prepare him for the Portland show in mid-July.

About an hour had passed and I was settled into my study working on a book manuscript when the phone rang. When I answered, I heard the panicky voice of Dog-mom. She was calling on her cell-phone.

"Hello, honey. I've got a problem here. I took Nike out of the van for a walk around the parking area where we are meeting The Source. When I got back to the van and tried to open the locked door with my electronic key, it wasn't responding to the signal. I think when you changed the battery last evening, it didn't get fixed properly. I don't know what to do."

I listened as she explained the situation. She and The Source called Triple A and learned that there were some difficulties opening doors on vehicles without the number of the electronic key.

I felt responsible for the whole situation and didn't hesitate to recommend my solution.

"Look, sit tight for a few minutes. There is an extra key in the drawer of my study desk. I've got it in my hand as we speak. I'm heading out the door right now. I'll be there in 45 minutes. See you then."

I terminated the call, turned off my study light and headed for the back door into the garage. Minutes later I was on the interstate heading north toward Albany. Dog-mom had given me the directions for where to exit the freeway and head eastward toward the fairgrounds. She was right in saying the direction was well-marked at the freeway exit.

I paid my three dollar daily admission to the parking area and headed to where the front entrance was to the fairgrounds. When I parked and started walking toward the gate I saw the relieved smile on Dog-mom's face. Nike was at her side on a leash.

"Thank you so much for coming, honey! I don't know how I would have gotten the van unlocked without this second set of keys."

I gave Dog-mom a reassuring hug and then followed her to where her van was parked. She pressed the key button and the doors unlocked.

Once she retrieved her purse, she re-locked the car and we headed for the fairground show arena building where the Bernese Mountain Dog competition was being held.

Dog-mom had Nike on a leash and he was well-behaved as we entered the large building. Dog-mom was unsure if it was proper protocol to bring a non-competing dog into the area, and I assured her nobody would know the difference—even though I didn't have a clue about what I was declaring in such a cavalier fashion. This was only the second time I'd entered the alien culture of dog show life!

We found the area of the building where the Bernese dogs were competing. There, sitting in a folding chair next to the three foot portable arena boundary fence was The Source. We greeted her and pulled up chairs so we could watch all the action.

Unlike the first show, I had the luxury of sitting next to The Source and she did her best to give me a crash course on what the judges were looking for as the handlers put the animals through their paces.

After the show, we took Nike to the grassy area outside the front entrance to the fairground building where the show was being held. There we met The Handler—an attractive middle-age woman dressed in a colorful, stylish sport coat and contrasting skirt. She was also wearing knee-high dark leather boots.

The initial meeting was quite cordial and brief as The Handler was on a break between two showings.

Dog-mom proudly held the leash of Nike and chatted with The Handler about what we wanted. Dog-mom's question was blunt and to the point. Did The Handler think Nike was mature enough physically and had sufficient attributes to groom him as a show dog?

The Handler walked away from us about five yards and told Dog-mom: "Walk him directly toward me so I can see how he gaits."

Dog-mom did as instructed. The activity was repeated several times. Finally, The Handler smiled and glanced at her wrist-watch. It was clear she was pre-occupied with her immediate task at hand—attending to an animal she was about to show in the afternoon completion.

"I think he is a good looking specimen. I always worry about young Bernese puppies because they have the tendency to have their hind quarters growing faster than their front—it gives an uneven back posture. Judges like to see a level spine—but that isn't always the case with puppies when they first start showing. Sometimes it only comes after they are mature—about two years old. But Nike is not bad. We'll see how he grows these next couple of months."

The Handler again glanced at her wrist-watch. "I'm willing to handle Nike. I'll be in touch with what is the best way to make the arrangements. As I understand it you and The Source want him ready for the big show in Portland in July. At that show he'll be old enough to compete in the 9 months to 1 year class. So I think we should have him get a little more experience working with me before then. I will get in touch with The Source and we can develop a suitable arrangement."

The Handler extended her hand toward Dog-mom and they shook hands politely.

Dog-mom wanted to return to the show area so I took my leave and headed to the parking lot.

I was delighted I was able to "save the day" by bringing the second set of keys to the show. It was my way of showing the love I had for Dog-mom! (We later learned, however, that there was a door lock key inside the electronic device that could be used in the event the electronic opener failed! Dog-mom was embarrassed she did not read the new owner's manual more thoroughly when we picked up the van from the dealership!)

The Albany show did open my eyes to all the fascination Dog-mom had with the curious show-dog culture. It was unclear to me whether Dog-mom was sold on the whole idea of displaying handsome dogs in competition based on looks, or whether the almost fanatical love and loyalty the other animal owners had for their pets fascinated her into wanting to be like them in sharing motherly pride in their four-legged-children.

For the next couple of weeks Dog-mom was in communication with both The Source as well as The Handler. I was the curmudgeon when it came to looking at the potential costs of the dog-show adventure. We certainly had the resources—financially and time-wise—but I wanted to make sure Dog-mom was aware and supportive of the cost of such an enterprise and whether it was a priority for how she wanted to spend the currency of her retirement life.

Dog-mom did her homework. I think she pestered The Handler for minute details and a formal contract for how much it would cost us to retain her as Nike's professional handler. The Handler was far more laid-back than Dog-mom when it came to such things— perhaps indicating the dog-show culture is more of a "gentle-persons" agreement than "business-like, contractual agreements."

Dog-mom finally had a good sense of the cost to retain The Handler and she had a good sense of the next step in the adventure. The Source indicated that the best way to make a transition from doing our own training of Nike would be to drive him over to Redmond, Oregon where The Handler was showing one of the other Bernese bred by The Source in a regional dog show.

There we could hand off Nike to The Handler and she would take him to her place in Washington and spend a week training him for how she liked dogs to behave when she showed them in competition. Her goal was to see how well he could be shown under her tutelage at the Centralia, Washington show. It was held two weeks before the big show in Portland and would be a good indicator of whether Nike was ready for Prime Time!

4

The Redmond Adventure

Taking Nike to a dog-show in Redmond, Oregon created mixed-feelings for Dog-mom. It was an hour-and-a-half trip up Highway 126 eastward through the McKenzie Forest past Sisters and then north 40 miles into the high desert of Redmond. It wasn't the time or the distance, but the realization she would have to return home from the trip without Nike in the van!

Truth be told, Dog-mom didn't feel comfortable weaning HERSELF from her seven-month-old puppy for a week. Since we had picked Nike up from The Source, he had not been out of Dog-mom's sight for more than a few hours.

Much to Dog-mom's credit, however, she sucked-it up and prepared herself for the inevitable—separation from her puppy! She packed Nike's bag like he was heading off for a one-week summer camp. There were hand measured plastic baggies filled with food portions to last him for the one week away-from home adventure. There was a bag of his favorite noise-making toys he liked to chew-upon. There was a bag off his special treats—as well as his favorite bones.

I actually looked forward to the trip because it was going to take me back to a portion of Eastern Oregon I had not visited for more than forty-years ago when I was in graduate school and took a group of students on a spring break symposium trip to do debates at service clubs in Eastern Oregon.

The portion of the trip that was through the McKenzie forest along Highway 126 was a route we had traveled several times since returning to Oregon three years ago. Our friends had a second-home in Black Butte and we made several trips there to enjoy their hospitality. It was only a few miles west of Sisters so we were familiar with that leg of the Redmond adventure.

Once we got east of Sisters, we turned and headed up to Redmond. I was pleasantly surprised at the spacious highway that led us through some beautiful open high plains that enjoyed spectacular views of the Three Sisters and other mountain peaks in the region.

When we arrived in Redmond we drove first to the fairgrounds where the dog show was set to be staged. Once we got the lay of the land, we drove to the motel where Dog-mom had made arrangements for our stay. It was, of course, a pet-friendly Motel 6. After we checked in we returned to the fairgrounds and connected with The Source as well as The Handler. They had a staging area in one of the indoor buildings of the fairgrounds.

The show itself was set up outside of the buildings. Fortunately, the weather cooperated and it was warm and almost balmy. Nike had no idea we were going to abandon him to The Handler after the event so he was very compliant when we put him in a temporary kennel so we could walk around the show and get the lay of the land.

Once again we were amazed at the cohesiveness of the dog-show faithful. There is clearly a culture of groupies who make a life-style of attending dog-shows and displaying their animals. Even after two shows I was beginning to recognize some common faces and dogs among the handlers and owners.

When we connected with The Source she took us into the grooming area where The Handler was preparing the dogs she would show the first day of the event. Afterwards, we took Nike with us and got some seats alongside the competitive arena so we could enjoy the show. Throughout the show we sat next to The Source and she educated us once again on the fine points of show-dog competition—always careful to interject the delicate variable of "judge politics" into the final scoring of each competition.

At the end of the first day, we returned to the motel. Dog-mom took Nike for a walk and business-making activity along the canal that ran behind our motel. Afterwards, we went to the room and waited for a phone call from The Source who was supposedly staying in our same hotel.

When dinner time approached and there was still no call from The Source about getting together, Dog-mom called The Source.

Dog-mom found out that The Source was staying in room 16—which Dog-mom realized was just down the hallway from us. She walked down the corridor and stood outside the door. Dog-mom was still on her cell-phone as she told The Source she was standing outside her door.

The Source was puzzled because on her end of the phone she was standing in her open door and couldn't see Dog-mom anywhere.

It was then both realized The Source was staying In Motel Eight a few blocks from the fairground. Dog-mom, husband, and Nike were staying in Motel 6—about two miles further down the road!

We laughed and laughed over the folly. When Dog-mom finally got composed and asked where everybody was gathering for dinner, we learned earlier that afternoon, The Handler had fallen and twisted her ankle while showing one of her dogs. She was resting in her room icing her elevated foot.

Dinner plans had obviously changed. The Source asked us if we could get some beer and pizza and we would have dinner in The Handler's room.

Dog-mom was delighted to be able to assist. We went to a nearby store and got a couple of six-packs of Fat Tire beer—a local favorite—a couple of large pizzas, then headed for Motel Eight.

Nike was a great sport in all the adventure. When we got to the motel we first went to the room of The Source. She had Nike's mom in her room. When Nike entered his mother Holly didn't recognize him or didn't care one way of the other. She simply growled and ignored him.

The Source said sometimes that is what happens so she kenneled her dog and we put Nike back in his kennel in our van. Then we went to The Handler's room where we enjoyed fellowship and consumed pizza and beer. Afterwards, we agreed with the Source we would pick her up at Motel Eight the next morning to go over to the competition.

The nice thing about our arrangements with The Source was that she could get up and see off The Handler as she went to the show with Holly. The Source could then enjoy a couple of hours extra sleep before heading over with us to the fairgrounds.

That next morning Dog-Mom and I went to a local restaurant for breakfast. We crated Nike in the van and enjoyed a peaceful start to the day. Then at about 9:30 we headed to the motel and picked up The Source. She was waiting for us in the lobby.

After the short drive from the motel to the fairgrounds, the Source instructed us on how to avoid parking far away from the action. We went to the side gate and told the attendant we were dropping a dog off for competition. She waved us through.

The Source smiled and told us, "At some of these shows you have to learn how to bend the truth. Once we get inside, I'll show you where you can park that will be directly next to the building where The Handler is grooming Holly!"

We enjoyed the afternoon showing of the Bernese. The Source's animal, Holly, did well and won in her class. During the show I formulated my own prejudices against various handlers. It was an emerging prejudice that proved to be quite valid—in my mind—in future shows we attended in Centralia and in Portland—but I am getting ahead of my story.

After the showing of The Source's dog Holly—Nike's mother—we took our leave of the event. We put the unsuspecting Nike into the designated Handler's kennel and quickly headed to our van, exiting the area of competition.

The drive back to Eugene was quiet. I tried to assure Dog-mom that her child would be fine. He was in good hands. And, it would only be a week before we would see him again in Centralia and have an opportunity to view how well he had been trained by The Handler.

Dog-mom was silent. It didn't matter how many positive images I painted with my word pictures about Nike enjoying summer camp. Dog-mom simply clenched her jaw and prepared for one of the longer weeks of her adult life.

5

Proper Show Dog Grooming

Dog-mom was somewhat familiar with the need to groom The Kid for the first dog show she entered him in at the Eugene Fairgrounds. She learned from Watson's mom of an up-scale dog-grooming service in downtown Eugene.

One Saturday morning I accompanied Dog-mom as she dropped off The Kid for an elaborate bathing and grooming. Ironically, the upscale boutique was co-owned and operated by the daughter of Ken Schilling, the no-nonsense trainer we originally connected with to help us with training Nike! It was an expensive visit—costing $80 dollars for a puppy. However, Nike's groomer was very skilled and Nike emerged as a well-groomed, handsome show dog ready for competition!

After she sent pictures of Nike to The Source, she was advised to connect with a woman who lived in the rural area of Albany East of Salem. The woman was a breeder who was more than willing to teach Dog-mom the fine art of grooming The Kid for dog shows.

Dog-mom had originally thought Groomer-Mentor would take about an hour of her time to show the proper techniques for grooming a Bernese for the show arena. She drove off with Nike at about 9:30 in the morning for the hour trip to Groomer-Mentor's home.

I began to worry as I looked up at the clock in my study later that afternoon. It was almost four o'clock and no Dog-mom. Finally I heard the sound of the garage door opening. Moments later Nike appeared at my study door, followed by Dog-mom.

Dog-mom was smiling and shaking her head. I knew there was a story about to unfold as Dog-mom headed for the kitchen for a snack—she had thought she would be home in plenty of time for lunch.

I followed Nike to the kitchen and leaned against the counter as Dog-mom scrounged through the refrigerator for some string-cheese and plate of apple slices she prepared earlier that morning.

"So, I take it from the looks of Nike that it was a successful lesson? He looks great."

Dog-mom took a deep breath and started her story.

"You are not going to believe what I experienced. Groomer-Mentor has a wonderful piece of acreage. There is a sprawling ranch-style home and plenty of room for her six Bernese Mountain Dogs to play and roam."

"Didn't you tell me she is an owner-breeder who shows her own dogs and doesn't use a professional handler?"

"Yes. The woman says she really enjoys doing everything—breeding, grooming, and handling the animals."

"How come it took so long? I thought you said she was going to give you an hour of her time?"

"That's what I thought. When I got there, however, she led Nike and I into a special room they added to their home. It is in effect a fully equipped dog grooming room where she had all the equipment arranged so she can bath and groom her Bernese. I couldn't believe how much time she spent bathing and brushing Nike and showing me special techniques she does to trim the ears and the feet of her show dogs.

"I take it she is a serious breeder and show-dog person?"

"Yes and No. She told me that I should consider continuing my training so I could handle Nike myself. She said her time in the show arena with one of her animals was the icing on the cake. She didn't want to share that experience with any professional handler."

"Did she convince you?"

Dog-mom paused before she answered.

"I don't know if I'm willing to get as involved as Groomer-Mentor is with the whole dog-show thing. I'm glad we are using a professional handler—especially for the big shows. I might consider handing Nike at small local shows—but I'm glad we have The Handler working with us to prepare for Nike's first big show."

I bent over and began rubbing Nike's chest. We had learned he preferred a chest and belly rub to us stroking his head and neck.

What he liked best, however, was rolling over onto his back and allowing someone to rub his belly! Bernese love belly-rubs!

As I rubbed his belly and talked to him in playful baby-talk that characterizes dog-mom and dog-dad talk I realized that it was going to be very interesting to see how Nike took to all this dog-grooming activity.

6

The Tumwater Event

The week without Nike between Redmond and Tumwater seemed like an eternity for Dog Mom. Each night when we went to bed, Dog-mom reminded me how much she missed Nike. Then the following morning she reinforced her misery by saying how strange it felt not to have Nike downstairs waiting patiently at the foot of the stairs for her to appear and greet him.

The day finally came when we packed our bag and headed to the dog show in Centralia, a neighboring city of Tumwater, Washington. My only recollection of the place was that decades ago when I was a child there was a television commercial that advertised Hamm's Beer with an animated cartoon bear and a catchy song that began with "From the Land of Sky Blue Waters."

I was suffering from an insect bite on my foot and one of my toes on my right foot was painfully swollen. Dog-mom's suggestion was to stop at the new Cabelas store in Springfield so I could get a pair of open-toed sandals. I agreed.

After about twenty-minutes in the store we emerged with my first pair of sandals in my adult life! I quickly realized how much more comfortable they were! After that we returned to the I-5 freeway and headed to Tumwater, Washington.

We would have arranged to stay in Centralia except there was a large bicycle race being held the same weekend as the dog-show in Centralia. As a result, there were no motel rooms available. The closest place where Dog-mom could find a room was in Tumwater, about 15 miles north of Centralia.

We had little difficulty finding the small but more than adequate motel. It was about four-thirty when we checked in and we were hungry. Dog-mom asked the clerk at the registration desk to recommend a good place to eat. She directed us to what she considered one of the best local restaurants.

As it turned out, it was located on a bluff that overlooked the river and was directly across the river from the famous old Hamm's Brewery of television commercial fame during my childhood. The brewery was now closed.

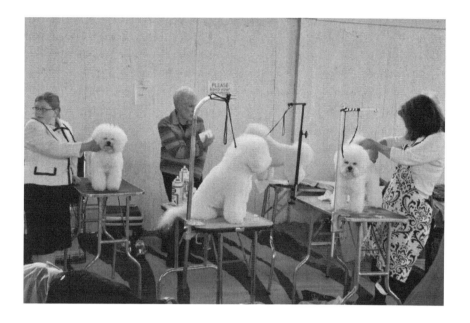

We were amazed at the spectacular view and enjoyed the ambiance of the restaurant. It has been on the same location for decades, but had been recently renovated and modernized and was a first rate venue for a restaurant.

After dinner we returned to the motel and retired early. We wanted to get around early so we could get some breakfast at the motel before heading down the freeway back to where we would exit I-5 for the Centralia Fairgrounds.

The trip only took us about twenty-five minutes to find the fairgrounds. We were surprised at how crowded the parking lot was as we approached the venue.

For five dollars we found a parking lot that was within easy walking distance to the covered outdoor arena where the dog-show was being staged.

We were especially concerned that we find a place to view the competition where Nike would not be able to see us. We took great care to avoid being in the entry way where Nike would be led into the competitive area. Dog-mom was concerned if he saw us before the show he would be distracted and not focused on The Handler.

We located The Source who was at the show because she was also showing Nike's mom and sister. She assured us that Nike was well-prepared for the competition. The Handler was confident in the results she had obtained by having Nike with her for the previous week at her home.

I confess I was most concerned about being out of the way so I walked to the far end of the covered arena where I was three competitive rings away from where Nike would be shown. It wasn't the best place to watch Nike perform, but it was the safest.

I held my breath when it was The Handler's time to bring Nike into the competitive arena. I watched in amazement as Nike went through the mandatory trotting and standing exercises. He did an outstanding job. I got a little teary when I realized that he was judged to be the best in his puppy category and was eligible to move to the next level of competition. In that level he got the second place Reserve ribbon.

Dog-mom and The Source were pleased with the results. Both agreed The Handler did what she was supposed to do to bring out the best in Nike.

After the showing we left the fairgrounds taking care not to be seen by Nike. We returned to Tumwater and the motel. That evening, Dog-mom thought about returning to the restaurant on the river where we'd eaten an outstanding meal the previous evening. I wasn't too keen on the idea and wanted to simply get something to eat nearby and turn in early so we could be rested and ready for the second day of competition.

As it turned out, when we left the motel we noticed there was a Mexican restaurant right across the parking lot of the Motel. I told Dog-mom I was game and would eat some gringo food if she wanted to enjoy the hot Mexican food that always caused my system to react to the spices.

It was a good food choice for both of us. About an hour we returned to the motel, watched some television—but both of us were pre-occupied with excitement and expectations for the second day.

The second day competition, however, was not meant to be. The Handler discovered what she thought was a hot spot forming on Nike's testicle area. Such a condition could well cause Nike to flinch and act out when a judge examined him during the competition. The Handler advised us against showing him the second day because she didn't want to risk imprinting on Nike's memory an adverse judge experience.

Even though we were disappointed, Dog-mom agreed with the judgment of the Handler. The Source was there when the decision was made and agreed it was best to pull Nike from the show.

Then Dog-mom was faced with the most difficult decision she had in Nike's short show-dog adventures.

Would it be best to leave Nike with The Handler for the next two weeks so she could take care of the hot spots and continue to prepare him for the big show in Portland or should Dog-mom take her child home for a week and then drive him back to Albany where the Handler would be showing another dog?

Originally, the plan had been to return to Eugene with Nike and then have him home for a week.

Dog-mom huddled with The Handler and The Source and they all agreed it would probably be best for Nike to stay with the Handler for the next two weeks. In that way The Handler could treat the hot-spot and get it healed. She could also continue to work with Nike as a show-dog team.

I could tell it was a tough decision—especially because Dog-mom would have to head home to Eugene without going by the crate in the grooming area where Nike was contained. We both took a deep breath and headed for our van.

But before the home trip we were able to meet the owners of Nike's sister, a female Bernese named Sooke II. We later found out that unlike Dog-mom's experience of waiting six months before going for a new dog after the former dog-child was put down, Sooke II's owners decided several days after the loss of their ten-year old Bernese that they wanted another pup. They connected with the Source to bring a new pup home within a short time so there was less empty nest grieving.

The other connection we made at the Centralia show was to see the Bernese that was the father of Nike's litter. He was a huge, handsome Bernese called Drako the dragon.. He was already experienced enough in the show-dog competition to have sufficient points to be considered a Champion dog.

After petting and admiring both animals, Dog-mom and I left the show without ever touching Nike.

The ride back to Eugene was a disappointing one not only because Nike was ailing and pulled from the second day of the show, but because we were not going to have his friendly puppy energy in our lives for another two weeks!

7

"The Summer Camp Void

Dog-mom was terribly disappointed that Nike didn't come home for a week but instead stayed with The Handler so she could work with him during the two weeks remaining before the big show in Portland.

But Dog-mom also completely understood it was the right decision for the time—especially since we were having a new patio roof built onto our home. Nike would clearly be in the way of saws, wet cement, ladders and electrical cords—all dangerous "toys" for the likes of Nike.

What was most disappointing, however, was Dog-mom's own decision not to take Nike home after the show, but to leave him in the charge of The Handler so she could work with him during the two remaining weeks before the big show in Portland.

I was amazed at how empty our home felt while Nike was being boarded and trained at The Handler's place.

We received assurances from The Source that Nike was doing well at his home away from home. In fact, to ease the angst of Nike's absence, I developed the habit of referring to his experience as his "summer camp" adventure. For me it eased the discomfort—but I can't say it did much to make Nike's dog-mom any more comfortable with his absence. It was clear the big guy had left a large, gaping hole in our everyday routines.

It didn't make much difference to Dog-mom. Nike was not with us and we felt a great void. As much as we tried to make light of the fact that Nike was at summer camp, it didn't really work for us.

Nike's dog-mom was constantly in touch with The Source—and at one point The Source advised her if she was so concerned about Nike's absence from our home, we should go and retrieve Nike and bring him home.

Fortunately, Nike's dog-mom was more objective. The summer camp void was necessary. She didn't like surrendering Nike, but she was going to be brave. Nike was, by all accounts, enjoying his experience at camp and was having a great time running with his sister in the dog runs!

But that didn't make it any the easier for Nike's dog-mom to deal with the absence of his everyday presence in our home.

Every day we spent without Nike was a reminder of how much the animal's presence was critical to our family life! A Dog-mom needs her dog! Period!

I was finally overjoyed when we were packing to go to the Portland dog show. It meant that we would be able to return home with our dog, regardless of how he performed in the show-dog world. He would be our everyday blessing!

8

Reflecting on Big Dog Mortality

Dog-mom had a lot to think about with the void created by Nike's absence. She was especially focused on the realization that Bernese Mountain Dogs were like all members of large-breed dogs especially prone to things like cancer. That is why the typical life-span is seven to eight years.

The relatively short-life span of the Bernese was underscored at one of the dog shows when there was a special tribute paid to the more mature competitors in the breed. Everybody watching the older animals enter the show ring gave special applause when the announcer proclaimed that the first Class-5 Bernese were nine-years old. The second Class were nine to eleven, and two of the dogs in the last Class contained one Bernese who was eleven years old!

Such a reality had been brought home to Dog-mom when Watson's mom phoned her and gave the news that Nike's great uncle, Watson—the BMD that attracted Dog-mom's attention in the parking lot of Jerry's Home Improvement Center and led to the eventual acquisition of Nike—was diagnosed with a cancerous growth on one of his front elbows.

On a prior occasion, we took Nike over to his great uncle Watson's house to meet and be around a more mature Bernese. Watson suffered Nike's puppy presence with dignity and decorum—but pretty much ignored Nike's overtures to be playful.

Watson was a six year old and the focus of attention of his retired school teacher mom. For a couple of weeks there was a flurry of e-mail activity between Dog-mom and her friend.

It was eventually decided that under no circumstances would Watson's mom consent to amputation as the means of preserving the remaining years of her child's life. Instead, she elected to have a protracted sequence of radiation treatment and follow-up chemo therapy to arrest the tumor.

Dog-mom admired the courage and fighting determination of Watson's mom as she drove everyday from Eugene to Portland for radiation treatment—a routine that required 20 consecutive visits excluding weekend.

Watson's mom was fortunate to have the companionship of her own adult mother to accompany her on most of the trips.

I really dreaded the reality of Watson's circumstances. I was, however, very supportive of the fact that Nike's Dog-mom was asked to accompany Watson's Dog-mom on two trips to Portland when Watson's dog-grand-mom was unable to make the trip.

Nike's dog-mom was honored to share with Watson's dog-mom's the journey to Portland. It was a wonderful way to continue sharing the bond that had formed when the two women met and talked about being dog-moms in the parking lot of Jerry's Home Improvement Center months earlier. Both had learned that dog-moms know things that ordinary moms fail to understand.

I recall the many conversations Nike's dog-mom and I had when she returned from the treatment Watson experienced. There was a great sense of family and gentle concern all the care-givers had as they helped Watson through his treatment protocols.

Everybody enjoyed and valued the gentleness Watson showed as he marched through his treatment regimen. They all relished the way Watson enjoyed his special treats after each treatments. They also realized how noble he was in receiving the lover and concern of each caregiver, too.

I was pleased to hear how Dog-mom shared her Christian values and beliefs to comfort her worried dog-mom friend. She wrote the following prayer and e-mailed it to her with the cover-memo that said:

"Carol—when words are hard to come by—this is how I lift Watson up to God for healing:"

Heavenly Father, I call on you right now in a special way.
It is through your power that Watson was created.
Your Word tells me You created ALL things—
Every breath he takes,
Every morning he wakes,
And every moment of every hour,
I know Watson lives under your power.
Father, I ask you now to touch Watson with the same power.
For if you created him from nothing,
You can certainly recreate him.
Fill Watson with the healing power of your spirit.
Cast out anything that should not be in him.
Mend what is broken.
Root out any unproductive cancerous cells.
Open and blocked arteries or veins and rebuild any damaged areas.
Remove all inflammation and cleanse any infection.
Let the warmth of your healing love pass through his body

To make new any unhealthy areas
So that his body will function the way you created it to function.
And Father, restore him to full health
In spirit and his body so that he can continue to enjoy a long,
loving
Life with his Mom, Carol.
I ask this through Christ our Lord.
Amen.

During the final months of Watson's life Dog-mom's care and compassion for her friend and her "child" was deeply anchored in her Christian beliefs.

And, in the final analysis, The sadness of Watson's death was softened by the realization that even though he is no longer physically with his dog-mom, he was healed and has returned to the peaceful presence of his Creator.

When Watson completed his treatment everybody wished him well in his recovery! But like all humans who know that the plan is not in their hands, they hoped that Watson would live as long as he was supposed to live.

And they were, in the final analysis, correct in their belief.

9

The Big Show

Dog-mom did not enjoy the reality that Nike was away for three weeks—it was clearly a barrier to future dog show competition if such a condition were required.

I have to admit I was kind of excited about the prospect of seeing how Nike would fare in competition with a large field of Bernese. Portland was going to be a watershed showing for Nike. We were told by both The Source and The Handler that Nike would probably best be kept from future showing until he fully matured as a two-year old. Portland would be a good test of how well he stacked up against the other competitive 9-12 month old Bernese.

One of the unintended benefits of acquiring Nike and engaging in the adventure of showing him in regional dog shows was the fact that we were finally having an opportunity to explore places in the Pacific Northwest we wanted to see. Even though we had been living in Eugene for better than three years, the Portland AKC Dog Show afforded us the first opportunity to have an over-night visit to the Portland area.

We arranged to stay at the Red Lion Inn on the Columbia River adjacent to the I-5 Bridge that spans the river into Washington.

When we arrived it was shortly after 1:30. We were surprised to find that several bus loads of young people were unloading. After we checked in we decided to have lunch in their restaurant. It was a spectacularly clear blue sky day. When we were seated we watched as a colorful paddle boat cruise ship glided up to the dock below the restaurant. We learned from the waitress that the ship was returning from a seven-day cruise up the Columbia River—though due to especially high waters the route had been altered this particular year. While we sat and enjoyed our lunch we were also treated to the raising of the highway draw-bridge that spans the river.

We were amazed at how quickly the section of the bridge was raised vertically so there was sufficient room for high-mast ships to pass under the bridge. The traffic was delayed a good fifteen-minutes while several boats took advantage of the passage. The waitress explained how the bridge was a terrible bottle-neck for locals who learned to work around the commute-time disruptions.

When we finished lunch Dog-mom decided we should drive over to the Portland Expo grounds to check out the place so we could know where to park and where to enter the building the next morning.

Unfortunately we chose the wrong time for such a trip. We went at the peak of the Friday afternoon rush-hour. The two-and-a-half mile loop took us the better part of an hour. We realized, though, that in the morning we would not have the same traffic congestion—and we had a good sense of where we wanted to park in the morning.

We drove around the hotel waterfront development for a few minutes before returning to the Red Lion parking area. When we pulled into the parking lot, Dog-mom's cell phone rang. It was The Source. She was calling to tell Dog-mom that the couple we were meeting for dinner had a mishap on the way down from their home in Washington. Their car broke down and they were having it towed to a dealership for repair. They were uncertain about dinner and would call us later.

Dog-mom volunteered to drive up and bring them down to the expo if necessary. We decided to wait and hear from the couple after they found out about their car and whether they could get a rental or a loaner car to continue on down to the expo. They were the owners of Nike's sister who was also being shown at the Portland event.

Fortunately, the couple was able to rent a car and meet us for dinner.

It was an enjoyable opportunity to get to know them better and to plan how we would get together again the next morning for the show. Dog-mom told them how excited she was to realize that after three weeks absence, she would be able to take Nike home after the show the next day. Nike's sister, Sooke II had also been boarded with The Handler for one week before the Portland show.

The next morning we were up early and enjoyed a hearty breakfast at the hotel restaurant before heading for the expo. When we arrived at the expo the show was already underway. Dog-mom's greatest concern was staying out of Nike's line of sight during the show and in between competitive displays.

We met up with Nike's sister's owners—Joe and Peggy and also connected with The Source. She informed us that The Handler was busy grooming Nike and his sister as well as rushing to several other showing of other dogs she was handling at the large event.

When it came time for Nike's performance, Dog-mom went to a place where she could photo The Handler putting Nike through his routine. I went across the large building where I could sit three venues away from where Nike would be shown. I could see The Source and the row of chairs we vacated so we wouldn't be a distraction for Nike. I had a good view as The Handler brought Nike into the arena.

I held my breath as Nike performed. He was remarkably well poised as The Handler jogged him through the routine. At the end the judge signaled to The Handler her dog won the blue ribbon! I waved at The Source who returned my wave with a thumbs-up signal.

During the time between Nike's first competition and his second round I watched the other contest taking place in another part of the building. It was the obedience training competition. I was amazed as the dogs not only went through a series of jumps, fetches, sits, and heel commands, but they were commanded to stay while their owners/handlers left the arena and the building. Each animal waited patiently for several minutes until their owner re-entered the building and returned to the side of their animal!

I did think this type of competition was better for the dog to do something it had learned and performed as a result of consistent training versus just "showing: a dog with good conformation to the breed physical standards. Oh well, who am I to know as a mere dog-dad!

After watching that competition, I walked back across the huge room in the arena where Nike was competing. I watched as a new judge compared Nike with many of the same dogs he competed against earlier. This time Nike was judged to be the runner up against the dog he beat in the previous showing! That, in a nut-shell seemed to sum up for me the curious thing about the dog-showing culture. While it may be a contest in which there are fixed standards that allow highly-trained judges to evaluate the relative merits of competing animals, there is never-the-less a great deal of subjectivity in selecting a winner. Some would say, too, that there are politics as well compounding the choice of a winner.

All in all, we were satisfied with Nike's performance and the results of his first big dog show. Dog-mom was still anxious about not being seen by Nike until we finished watching the other dogs that had been bred by The Source who were being shown at the Portland Show. By contrast, I was fatigued by what I considered the highly redundant activities that occupied our attention from our 9:00 AM arrival time until the current 3:30 PM time. I was impatient and ready to take Nike home now that his competition was complete.

Dog-mom prevailed by insisting she wanted to get a professional photo taken by the photographer to memorialize Nike's first major dog show victory in his class. Dog-mom knew it would be the last major show for at least a year or so until Nike was more fully mature.

Deg-mom was also concerned about how Nike would respond to her when she finally appeared to leash him and lead him out to our van. She waited patiently while the photographer posed Nike on the award stand with the judge as well as The Handler.

When the photo was complete, The Handler brought Nike down from the award stand and over to the side of the crowd watching the photos of the award winning dogs.

Dog-mom had Nike's collar and a leash. At first when Dog-mom started to put the collar around Nike he didn't realize who was performing the task. Then, as if he finally recognized her smell, Nike went into a fit of joy as he tucked his head between her legs as she crouched down to affix the leash. He climbed over her shoulders and rubbed his body against Dog-mom in what must have seemed to on-watchers as if the dog was having some kind of epileptic seizure!

If Dog-mom had any doubts about whether she was missed or whether her child would recognize her after three-weeks at doggy-camp with The Handler, her worries were put to rest immediately as Nike celebrated the re-union.

Dog-mom finally got Nike under control and we said our goodbye's to The Source and the Handler and our new friends, the owners of Nike's sister—who, by the way did well in the show with a first place in her completion as well.

Dog-mom drove the van home. I was exhausted from a lack of sleep the night before as I struggled with first-night adjustments to a new sleeping situation. Nike was exhausted, too, from all the activity and stimulation of the Portland show. He made no resistance when Dog-mom open the door of his crate and tossed in a treat to encourage him to enter.

It was nice to be returning to Eugene and to allow Nike to resume his role as a normal, nine-month old family dog!

It still remains unknown how much of his future would be spent in the glamour of a show-dog arena. One thing was certain—there would be plenty of time before he would subjected to the rigorous routine that took him away from Dog-mom for three-weeks.

10

"Growing Pains!"

I have to constantly remind myself that Nike is not yet a year old. He is adult size with a puppy mentality. Case in point is how he behaved recently when we returned home after Church. He was roaming in the house and found the television remote. When Dog-mom went into the back yard she found it scattered all about the yard. At first she was concerned the batteries might have been ingested. Fortunately, none of the debris was ingested. I was angry and went off in a huff to replace the remote. I went to the Comcast offices and found out that it wasn't their device, but the other one we used to adjust the volume.

On the way home from Comcast I stopped at a television store and asked the clerk if there were such thing as a generic all-in one remote. He sold me the state of the art device that required me to go on line and program the device. It was a tedious task but once it was done the silver lining in the Nike mischievous act was the reality it forced me to finally get a single device to operate the television. That reality made the mishaps less of a nuisance.

It was only a day or two later, however, when Nike again struck. I accidentally left the door to my study open when Dog-mom and I went on an errand. When we got home I discovered Nike had purloined from my desktop my computer mouse. It was out in the grass and quite nicely chewed-up beyond use!

I was able to find a replacement for the remote wireless mouse and my computer-centered writing world was repaired.

I realize that when Nike is bored he looks for things to get into—almost as though he were punishing us for not attending to his needs. He so enjoys moving stealth-like through a room and snatching a napkin from someone's lap at the dinner table and then hustling to the other room stopping only momentarily to make sure his stunt had attracted Dog-mom's or my attention!

It used to be easy for Nike to poke his head through our legs and show his affection by slipping through our legs—often turning and catching his own tail and then circling one leg with the tail firmly grasp in his mouth.

Not that he is growing more vertically, this playful way of showing affection is more difficult!

One of the great things about Nike is how well he has adapted to making long trips in the van. Nike was only with us for four days before we packed him into the van and made the seven hour trip down to Paradise to visit with Dog-mom's mother. Every hour or so we pulled into a rest-stop and allowed Nike out of his crate to walk around, sniff and do his business.

Nike has learned to relish the long trips. We no longer fret over whether he considers it punishment to be put in his crate. He often spends hours sleeping comfortably in the huge crate we have for him. He has become accustomed to stopping every couple of hours at the wonderful I-5 rest-stops. Whenever we stop many fellow travelers stop and admire our handsome dog—often confusing him with their perception of a St. Bernard.

As Nike works through is puppy growing pains, his Dog-mom is also being taught lessons about what he can be trusted to do when left along in her van. One Sunday, for example, we decided to leave him along in the van in the church parking lot while we went into the sanctuary to listen to the pastor's sermon. An hour and a half-later when we returned, Dog-mom was shocked to find he had chewed on the back of the driver's seat—causing several hundreds of dollars of damage!

We drove immediately to Pet Smart and purchased the largest hard-shell crate and had the clerk put in the back of the van! It has become the safe place for Nike to rest and avoid the temptations of puppy mischievous behavior that befalls a bored puppy when left unattended in a vehicle!

We continually find that as Nike grows he has developed the habit of "counter-surfing." This means that anything we place on a counter that is reachable is in his mind fair game. Deb's bible was recently the source of one of Nike's explorations—she found the leather-covered, zippered book on the back yard lawn—evidence that he, too, was curious about the word!

One of Nike's favorite habits is finding the pantry door in the kitchen cracked open. When we commit that error, Nike is very stealth and grabs the trash bag and pulls it out to the back yard lawn where he explores its contents and displays his results for us to discover when we return home.

Nike is also greatly interested in all the tools and utensils I use when I use our outdoor grill. Most of the appliances have evidence that he has enjoyed chewing on them when they are accidentally left out for him to procure!

Anyone time there is a stranger at the front door Nike is on the spot to greet them and make sure they acknowledge he is present. In a sense, both Dog-mom and I have grown accustomed to dealing with the growing and maturing of Nike.

Whenever I find myself frustrated with some mess he has made, or some behavior that is annoying, I remind myself that for Nike life is indeed short—and we should relish all the good moments we share with him as he demands our attention and love—and in return finds ways to bring smiles to our faces.

11

"Dog's Die"

And, so I return again to the stark reality that faces all Dog-moms. Dog's moms know they will most probably bury their children— and many like Nike's Dog-mom will bury generations of children.

It comes with the territory. That's why Dog-moms must be strong. They must come to the realization that their children are dependent upon them to know when it is "their time."

I am among those who believe there is no such thing as a coincidence in life—all things are interrelated and serve small parts in God's grand scheme of things.

It was only several weeks ago that Dog-mom's good friend and our neighbor who lives next door to us in Aptos called Dog-mom and emotionally shared the reality that she had finally gathered the strength to put-down her infirmed Standard Poodle named Blue.

Blue was acquired by his dog-mom weeks after we got our second Golden retriever—Luke—to be a companion dog for Toby.

For the better part of a decade Blue took frequent walks with Dog-mom as she took her two children to the park at the bluffs that overlooked the Monterey Bay.

Blue's dog-mom knew that Nike's dog-mom would be a source of comfort during her grief. Nike's dog-mom had less than a year earlier experienced the same grim reality that comes with being a loving dog-mom.

What Nike's dog-mom didn't realize, however, was how soon after losing her beloved Blue, that her dog-mom would again find the courage to start again a love affair with a new dog-child.

When we returned to our former home recently, Dog-mom was anxious to see her old friend and to give her comfort and support for her great loss. She also wanted to share with Blue's dog-mom the joy that Nike had brought back into her life after the death of Luke.

Nike's Dog-mom was absolutely stunned when she called Blue's Dog-Mom and learned she had been "smitten" by another dog. It wasn't a puppy, but it was a three-year old dog.

What was incredible was the mixed breed she was considering adopting. It was half-Standard Poodle like her beloved Blue. The other half was—I kid you not—a Bernese Mountain Dog just like Dog-mom's Nike!

Blue's dog-mom has yet to acquire the new child, but the woman and her husband passed the first test and will most probably receive the new animal in the next few days!

The entire drive home from Aptos to Eugene I often flashed on how curious it was that Blue's Dog-mom now has a new child that is half poodle and half Bernese!

The reality of life continuing on for Dog-moms was brought home when we arrived back in Eugene. There was an e-mail waiting for Nike's dog-mom. It was from her new friend and fellow-dog-mom—the mother of Watson—the Bernese that caught Nike's dog-mom's attention that day at the Home Improvement Store parking lot.

Nike's dog-mom was aware that Watson's Dog-Mom had recently been through a lot of anxiety as she took her six year old child to Portland for daily radiation and chemical treatments for a cancerous condition on one of his front paws. On several occasions Nike's dog-mom accompanied Watson's mom on the two hour drive up for the treatment. Hopes were high that the treatment would buy a lot of quality time for the recovering Bernese.

(The photo above deserves a sub-title as it represents the first time puppy Nike met Watson and his Dog-mom.)

The e-mail brought tears to our eyes as Nike's Dog-mom handed me the print-out she could not bring herself to read aloud to me. It read as follows:
Watson's Mom here.

This morning we took my Boy into Bush Animal Hospital.

He is no longer in pain.

All of the techs, docs, and receptionists had the opportunity to say goodbye to him.

He's been almost totally pain free except for these last few days. Yesterday, when we were laying on Mom's couch, he stretched his head up and laid it on my chest. Our eyes met for a long time, and his look seemed to say, "I'm sorry Mama but I'm really tired. Can you help me?" Today, when we were laid together, I gave him that help with tears and words, "I will always love you—forever."

So I have to feel that the Good Lord said, "If you want me to heal him, you must give him to me!"

He's healed totally now with my Dad at the Rainbow Bridge along with Grandma Pat, Lexi, Neo and his other sisters.

We thank you for all your prayers and good wishes. They were answered. Not in the way we wanted but in the way they needed to be.

Of course there is a HUGE empty hole in Mom's heart and mine. As Bev told me on the phone, and I hope I got this right Bev,

Every time you lose a dog, you lost a big part of your heart. Every time you get a dog, they give you a big part of their heart. If we are very lucky we will be blessed to have the heart of a dog.

Love your Fur babies for Watson and us.

Carol and Myrna.

I don't know how Watson's dog-mom will bring closure to her loss. I know that Bernese dog-moms are a sturdy group of folks.

In fact, there is some sense that Watson's Dog-mom will connect with The Source and perhaps enjoy the experience of helping with the birth of the next litter The Source's dog produces. I wouldn't be surprised, either, if Watson's Dog-mom comes away from the experience with a new puppy of her own. That's the kind of strength a Bernese Dog-Mom has that gets her through the rough days of grieving.

Such evidence of the strength of a Bernese Dog-mom was brought to our attention when we met the owner's of Nike's sister, Sooke II. Her Dog-mom did not let any sizeable time lapse between losing their former Bernese and acquiring Sooke II from the same litter where Nike's dog-mom acquired him!

A Dog-mom's life is rich with many blessings—not the least of which is the daily reminder of what it means to enjoy unconditional love.

Any animal who is fortunate enough to live a lifetime with a dog-mom already has a good sense of what heaven is all about!

Living with a dog-mom as a partner is as good as it gets for any human—and is probably the next best thing to being a beloved dog!

Dog mom's are always not far away from a camera when it comes to capturing and documenting the cute moments of their children's behavior. Nike's Dog-mom is no exception. The pages that follow are evidence that a Dog-mom is every alert for the precious moments that a camera lens can capture in their child early years of life.

October 22 was the birth of Nike's litter. The first year's journey is evidenced by the pictures that follow. It has been a wonderful first year and we relish the thought of having many more days with Nike—and like our own human journey, we take each a day at a time.

12

The Post-Script

Nike continues to occupy a central role in the life of Dog-mom—and we both look forward to the life he will share with us—however brief it may be.

It was interesting how when we made the decision to have another "child" during our retirement years we received a great deal of push-back from Dog-mom's sisters. They were genuinely puzzled about our decision to adopt a new child now that we were both over sixty and poised to enjoy our good retirement years of travel and self-focus on completing our "bucket lists" of activities and things we wanted to do before we die.

I obviously had a different take on the situation. Who is more capable of giving love and attention and focus to the needs of a young puppy than a retired couple?

And, who is more appreciative of the love and attention a dog can give its master than someone who has "been-there-done-that" for a life-time of human experiences that accompany a successful professional career, countless vacation experiences at home and abroad, and many fond memories of past relationship with loving dogs.

I look at Dog-mom's daily activities and enjoy the routine she has established with Nike during this first year of his life.

Each morning he greets her joyfully at the bottom of our stairs as she descends to begin the day. I know she often rises at an early pre-dawn hour to spend some quiet time on her computer in her study before turning her attention to the wants and needs of her child.

Nike is now a year old and he has grown taller and longer than his earlier puppy days. When he greets Dog-mom in the morning he puts his huge paws on her shoulders and he licks her face and ears as she embraces him and looks him in his eyes lovingly and stands upright before her!

I have to remind myself he is still a puppy inside, regardless to the maturity of his physical body.

Nike has become accustomed to going to a local dog-park on Royal Avenue here in Eugene. It is about a 15 minute drive from our home.

Several times a week Dog-mom quickly gets around with a cup of coffee and prepares Nike's breakfast—two and a half cups of kibble stirred with a half container of yogurt!

He is usually too excited at the thought of going to the park to run with his dog friends that he only consumes a part of the food before he barks and whines. It is his "hurry up mom" vocabulary.

It usually works. Dog-mom opens the door into the garage and uses her van remote to open the sliding door into the back of the van. Nike wastes no time scrambling into the back and sitting impatiently while Dog-mom climbs into the driver's seat with her cup of coffee and raises the garage door.

The times I have accompanies Dog-mom on this morning ritual I am always amused by Nike's antics. He literally can barely contain himself as Dog-mom heads for the park. He sits with his head between Dog-mom and me and watches to make sure he sees the familiar landmarks that indicate we are indeed heading for the Royal Avenue dog park.

The closer we get to our destination the more difficult it is for Nike to be calm. He often raises his head back and almost sounds like a hunting hound as he bays and make little high pitched squeals of delight that are often piercing to the human ear!

When Dog-mom arrives at the park she almost wrestles with her child to get his leash connected to his collar so they can walk across the street to the entrance to the park. Dog-mom has commented that it is getting more difficult to control the powerful pull of her excited child as they reach the gate and enter the park.

Most mornings, Dog-mom tries to get to the park by 8:15 to 8:30. She has found that several other dog-moms bring "nice" dogs to the park. Only occasionally does Nike encounter a less than playful dog—and fortunately Dog-mom is there to referee and make sure no harm comes to her child from a bullying, aggressive playmate.

Nike wastes no time when he is unleashed to find a group of playmates to cavort with and chase around the fenced grassy acreage of the park.

It is not uncommon for Nike to run and chase other dogs for twenty-five or thirty minutes—which is more than sufficient vigorous exercise for a puppy his size. Dog-mom always worries that he is so big and powerful that he might accidentally hurt himself or another dog as they get their legs tangled in the excitement of the chase.

I consider the dog park analogous to taking a young child to the playground where parents supervise the play of their children and allow them to learn the norms of appropriate social behavior.

In the more recent months Dog-mom has realized that her uncut male child is now becoming more driven by his hormones that he was earlier in his puppy life. Now when he goes to the dog park he is more than eager to chase all the female dogs—whether they are in heat of not! Dog-mom is resolved to be more careful in controlling the natural instincts of Nike.

I liken it to the earlier day of my own childhood when during recess we would chase the girls and they would flee into the sanctuary of the girls' restroom for a safe respite from the chasing activity!

When Nike is done with the morning activity he is usually exhausted and ready for the rest of Dog-mom's shopping and errand running activity. He is more than cooperative in crawling into his kennel in the back of the van and enjoying down time accompanying Dog-mom and simply being with her.

In recent months the dog park experience has reinforced Dog-mom's realization that dog-children need companionship of other dogs. Dog-moms are cool, but having another dog in the family relieves a single child of the boredom that can accompany the time spent alone in the backyard finding things to occupy one's time when there is not a Dog-mom of dog-dad present to entertain.

One of the other routines Nike has developed this first year of his life's adventure is the habit of coming into my study and asking for attention. I normally am at the keyboard of my computer working on a writing project. Nike wanders in from the backyard and sits at the side of my desk waiting to make eye-contact and extending his paw so I can shake it.

After I stroke his chest and shake his hand he plops to the floor as though he is going to rest next to me. Instead, he edges himself slowly under my desk until he can bury his head in my waste basket and get his mouth around some discarded papers. The moment this happens, he snatches the papers and races toward the door—hoping he has something I want and am willing to chase him out the back door into the yard.

Occasionally, if the plastic wastebasket is empty, he will grab the edge of the basket and carry it in his mouth out to the yard where he will sprawl out on the grass with the basket clenched firmly in his mouth—waiting with an impish look on his face for me to approach him. When I do, he is off to the races! He jumps up and carries the basket to the other end of the yard—and again sprawls on the lawn awaiting my approach!

When I want to end the play it is necessary for me to go to the "cookie jar" Dog-mom keeps filled on the kitchen counter with dog-snacks. I get a small chicken strip and return to the yard where I allow Nike to extort it from me in exchange for the treat!

This activity is Nike's way of relieving the boredom that comes from being an only child.

I suspect many readers who have dog-mom experience know where this is leading.

Yes, Dog-mom and I are now giving serious thought to adding a second Bernese child to our family—perhaps as early as this next spring!

Anyone who has seen how Nike is growing into a powerful, energetic dog that is time consuming and demanding of attention would be justified in thinking this middle-aged retired couple have gone off the deep end. But only a true dog-mom knows there is indeed a method in such perceived madness!

Even though two big dogs represent an additional challenge, Dog-mom knows from our previous experience with our beloved Golden Retrievers that a companion dog is literally a God-send when it comes to meeting the needs of a single dog's needs.

We have begun the discussion with The Source about acquiring another puppy from one of her next litters. This time our motive is different than it was with Nike.

Dog-mom is more focused on the companion role of the next child—and is interested in getting a small female that we can have fixed and treat as a family dog and not a show animal like Nike.

Will such a decision drastically alter our retirement plans? No! I agree with Dog-mom's assessment that it can actually make our lives less stressful knowing that when we leave the home we will not feel guilty that Nike is along—but has the presence of another animal. When we go to the dog park we will bring a playmate for Nike to enjoy when there are no other dogs in the park. When we take Nike for walks through our tiny neighborhood both Dog-mom and I will have a loving family member at the end of a leash. When we visit family and friends we will do as we have done with Nike and joyfully include both animals in our plans.

One of the great blessings of being a Dog-mom is the reality that there never has to be an "empty-nest." There can always be present a child that needs and wants the loving attention of its Dog-mom. With two dog children, however, there can be less stress on Dog-moms than the responsibility of being present for a single child 24/7!

And, though I am with tongue-in-cheek, I can remind Dog-mom that two animals will provide her with twice the opportunities to capture for future photo albums and books picture of her beloved four-legged children.

We love you, Dog-mom!

13

Photo Gallery

You can never have enough photos of your human children to document the precious moments of their lives. Nike's Dog-Mom is not only proud of her four-legged children, but she is also an avid and talented photographer in her own right.

The following photos speak for all the moments in Nike's first year of life where Dog-Mom has been on hand to capture photos that display the many dimensions of her handsome child's personality.

This chapter is intended to provide other dog-moms (and dad's) with some additional visual evidence of the wonderful relationship between Nike and Dog-Mom!

The photo are in no specific order nor are they organized around any special event or themes—they simply represent Dog-Mom's having her camera eye on her child for most of the first year of Nike's life. Enjoy!

(This is Drako, the champion father of Nike—it was the day at the Portland dog show when he won best in breed!)